BUILDING BLOCKS OF BIOLOGY

THE CELL

Written by Jeff De La Rosa

Illustrated by Ruth Bennett

www.worldbook.com

Co-published by agreement between Shi Tu Hui and World Book, Inc.

Shi Tu Hui
Room 1807, Block 1,
#3 West Dawang Road
Chaoyang District, Beijing 100025
P.R. China

World Book, Inc.
180 North LaSalle Street
Suite 900
Chicago, Illinois 60601
USA

© 2026. All rights reserved. This volume may not be reproduced in whole or in part in any form without prior written permission from the publisher.

WORLD BOOK and the GLOBE DEVICE are registered trademarks or trademarks of World Book, Inc.

Library of Congress Control Number: 2025942735

Building Blocks of Biology
ISBN: 978-0-7166-6737-7 (set, hard cover)

The Cell
ISBN: 978-0-7166-6739-1 (hard cover)

Also available as:
ISBN: 978-0-7166-6759-9 (e-book)
ISBN: 978-0-7166-6749-0 (soft cover)

WORLD BOOK STAFF

Editorial

Vice President
Tom Evans

Senior Manager, New Content
Jeff De La Rosa

Proofreader
Nathalie Strassheim

Graphics and Design

Senior Visual Communications Designer
Melanie Bender

Acknowledgments
Writer: Jeff De La Rosa
Illustrator: Ruth Bennett/The Bright Agency

TABLE OF CONTENTS

Fur's New Pet 4

Parts of the Cell 8

Science Fun with Fur:
Make Your Own Pet Ameba 12

Root's Laboratory 15

Cellular Digestion 17

A Shrinking Problem 20

Animal Cells 22

Organelles 24

Plant Cells 28

Cell Division 30

Life on the Edge: Stem Cells 32

Show What You Know 38

Answers and Words to Know 40

There is a glossary on page 40. Terms defined in the glossary are in type **that looks like this** on their first appearance.

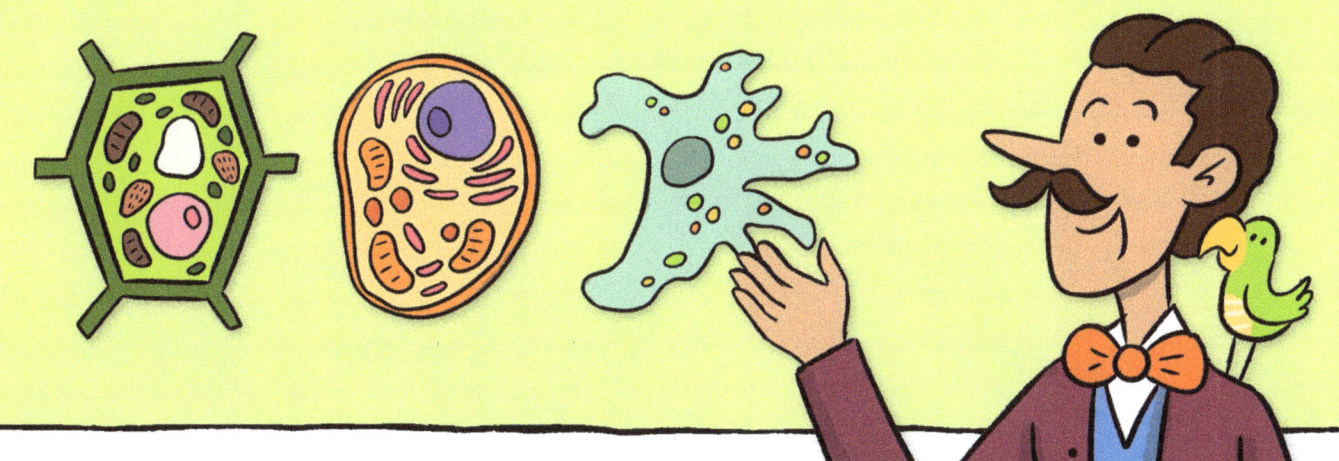

I don't see anything!

Of course, you don't!

An ameba is a single living **cell**... and cells are tiny.

PLANT CELL   ANIMAL CELL   AMEBA

All living things are made of cells...

...including plants, animals, and even you.

Even this little gecko has billions of cells.

But, some living things only have one...

Like your new pet, here.

I bet none of your friends have a pet ameba!

It looks kind of... sick.

No, the clerk at the pet store explained everything.

This outer covering is called the **cell membrane.**

STREEEEEEEEETCH

It's like the "skin" of the cell—it keeps the insides in and the outsides out.

This gooey stuff on the inside is called **cytoplasm.**

It fills up the body of the cell.

SCIENCE FUN WITH FUR!

MAKE YOUR OWN PET AMEBA

YOU WILL NEED:
- a sturdy plastic bag, like a freezer bag
- a jar or other container of similar size to the bag
- a rubber ball
- powdered gelatin
- heavy tape, like duct tape

WARNING: This could get a little messy...
Ask an adult for permission before starting!

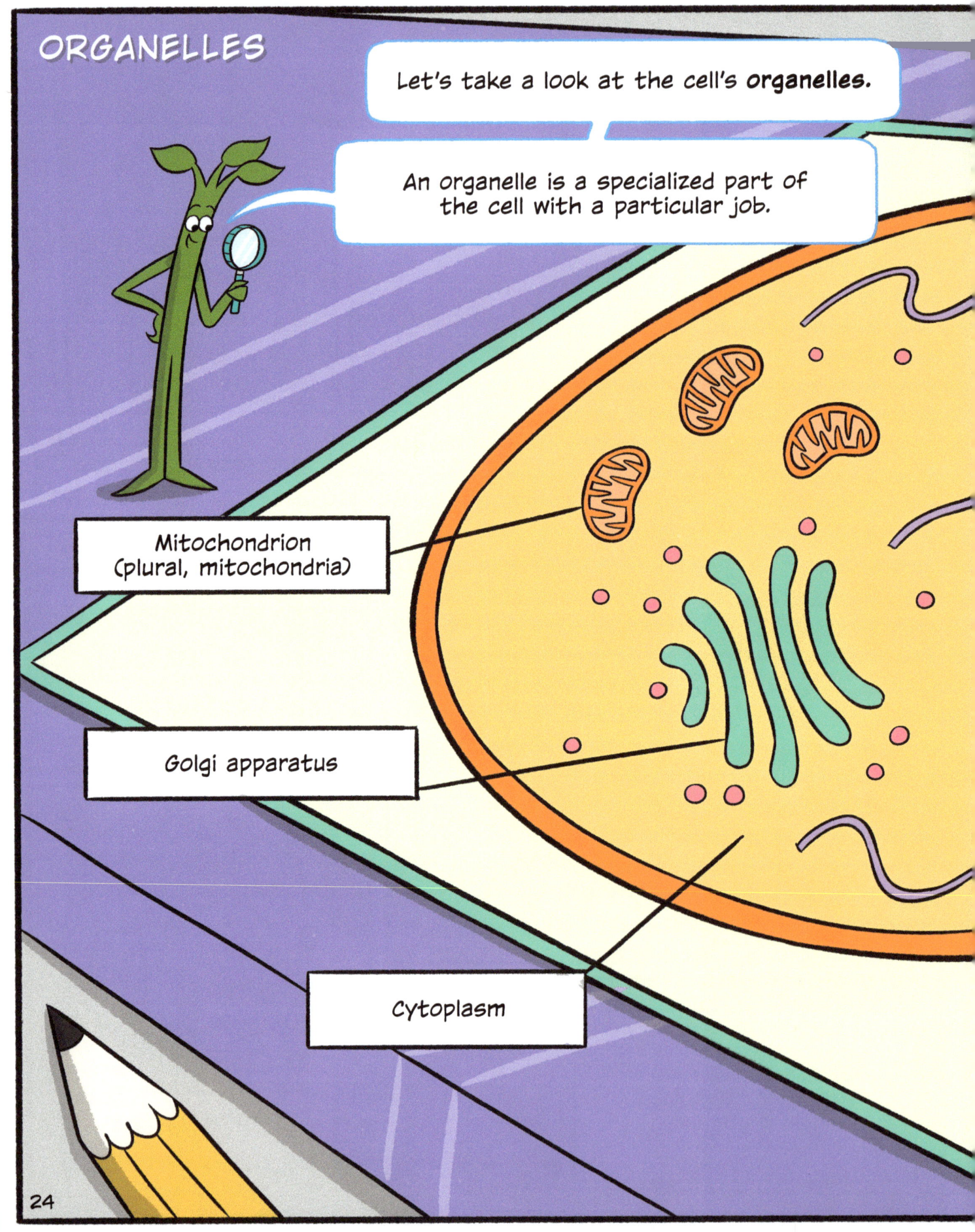

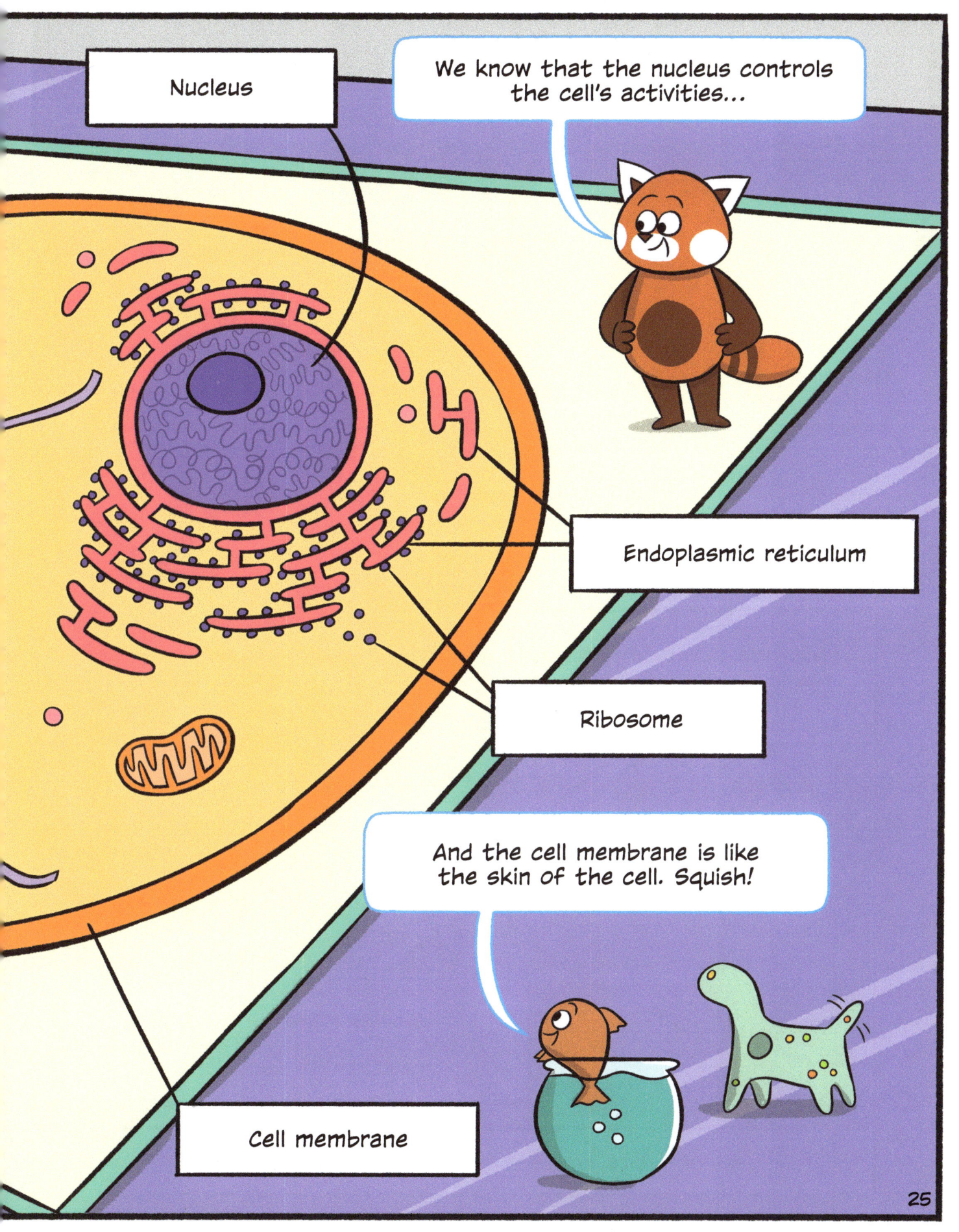

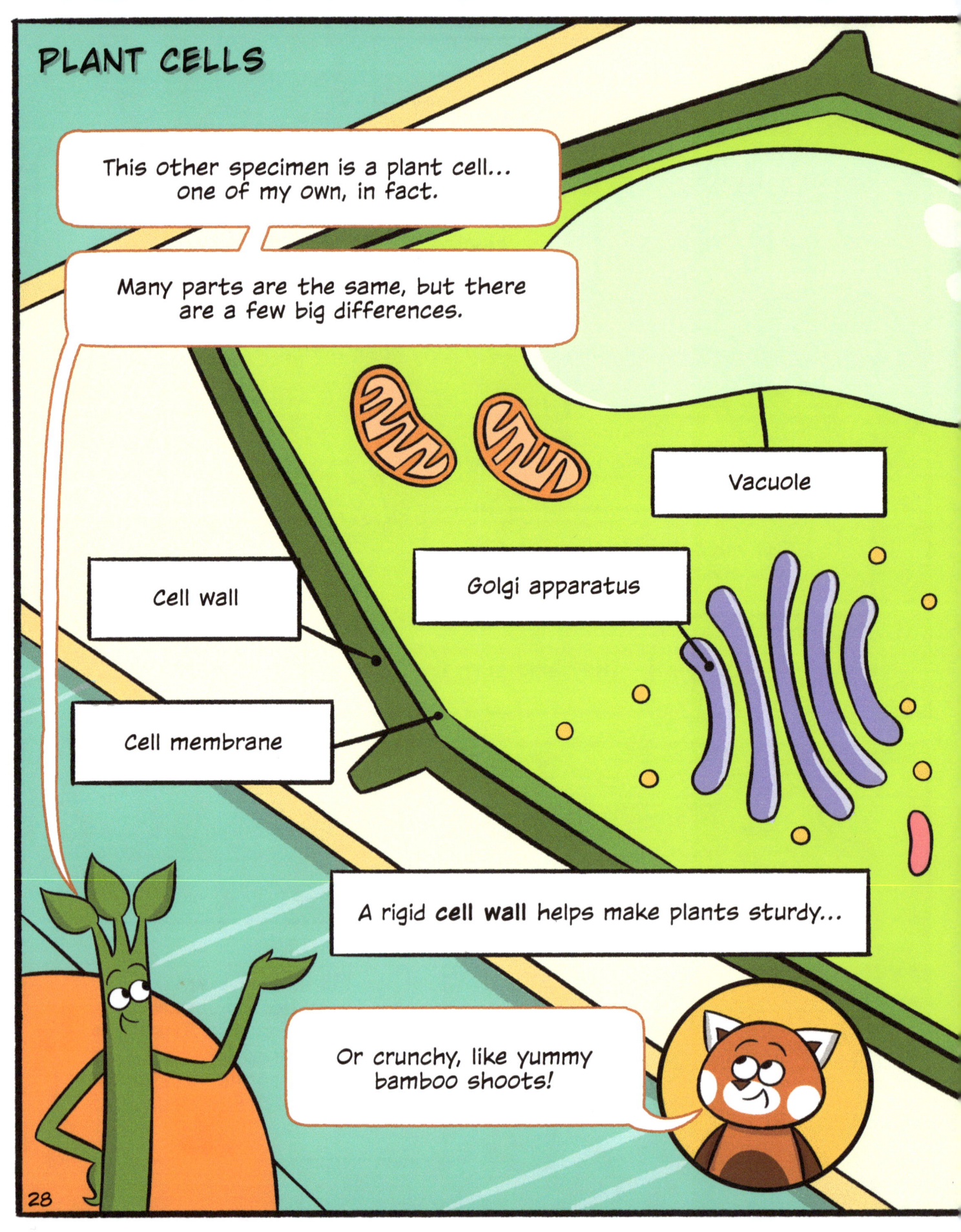

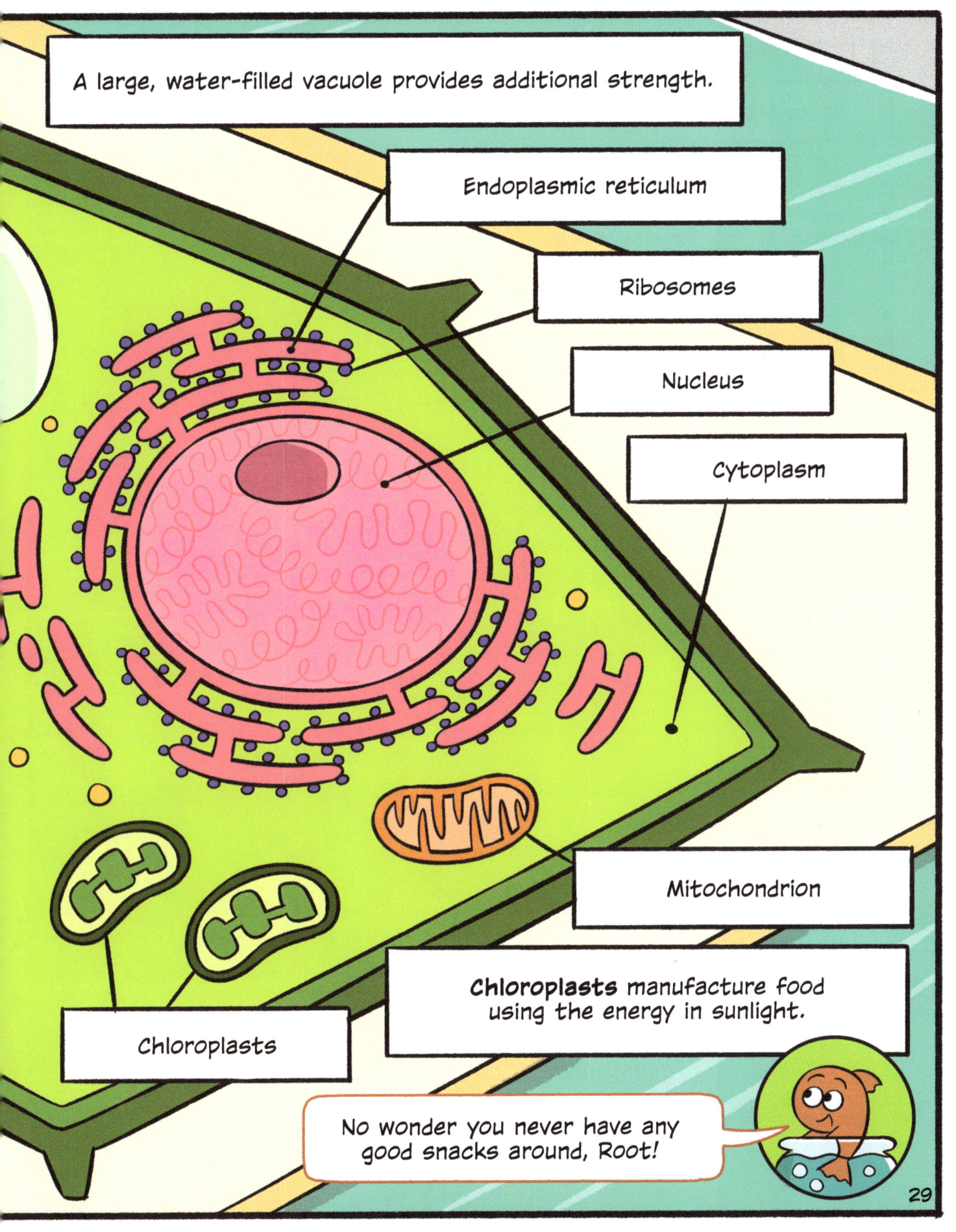

Each cell type is specialized for a particular function.

PLAYER 2 : SELECT CELL TYPE

BONE CELL

Bone cells build and maintain the skeleton.

Red blood cells carry oxygen in the bloodstream.

RED BLOOD CELL

FAT CELL

Fat cells store energy for later use.

Skin cells cover and protect the body.

SKIN CELL

MUSCLE CELL

Muscle cells use long, strong fibers to move the body.

WHITE BLOOD CELL

NERVE CELL

White blood cells attack and destroy germs.

Nerve cells transmit electrochemical impulses that coordinate body functions.

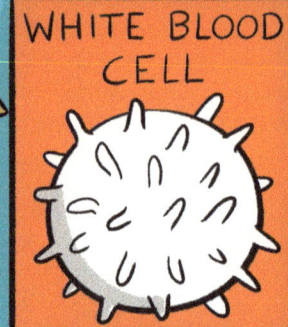

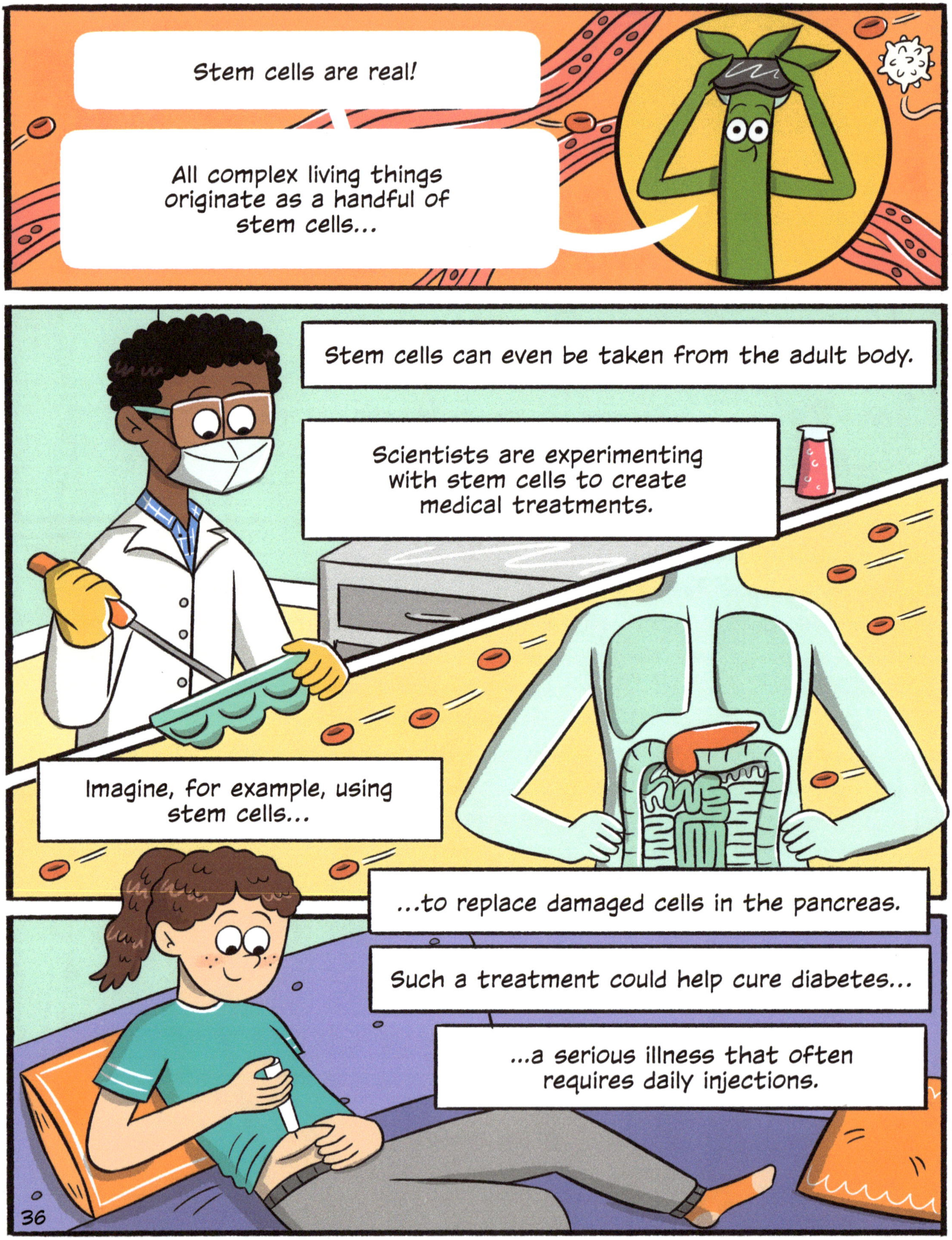

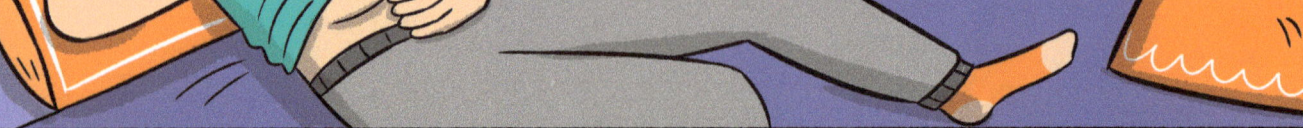

SHOW WHAT YOU KNOW

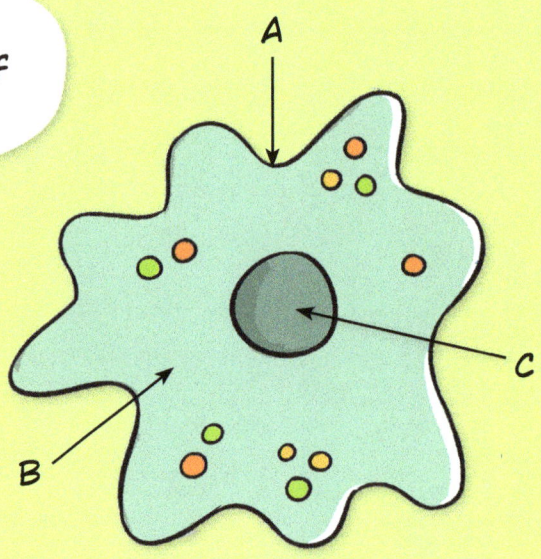

1. Identify these parts of the cell.

2. Match each cell part to its function.

chloroplast
lysosome
mitochondria
endoplasmic reticulum

A. powerhouse of the cell
B. make food using the energy in sunlight
C. carries digestive chemicals called enzymes
D. manufacturers proteins through the activity of ribosomes

3. Which of the following are found in plant cells but not animal cells?

cell membrane
cell wall
chloroplast
mitochondria
nucleus

4. Fill in the blanks.

A. The _____ _____ is like a tiny post office. There, proteins are packaged into sacs called _____ for delivery around the cell.
B. An ameba moves by reaching out with a _____ .
C. _____ _____ can turn into other types of living cell.

See page 40 for answers.

ANSWERS

page 11: nucleus; cytoplasm

page 19: vacuole; lysosome; enzymes

page 27: proteins; ribosomes

page 31: cell division

SHOW WHAT YOU KNOW ANSWERS pages 38-39:

1. A. cell membrane
   B. cytoplasm
   C. nucleus

2. A. mitochondria
   B. chloroplast
   C. lysosome
   D. endoplasmic reticulum

3. 3. cell wall, chloroplast

4. A. Golgi apparatus; vesicles
   B. pseudopod
   C. stem cells

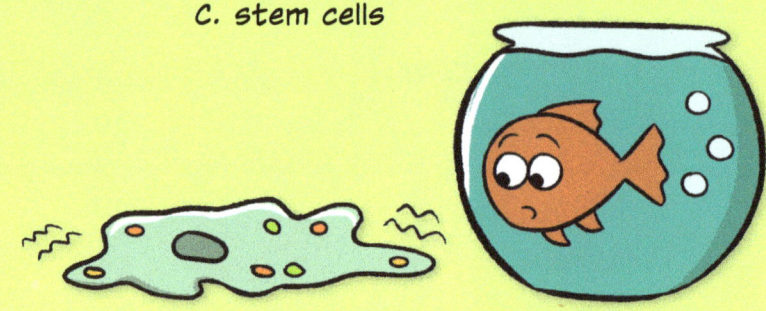

WORDS TO KNOW

cell the basic unit of life. All living things consist of one or more cells.

cell division the process by which cells split in two to make more cells.

cell membrane the thin, flexible covering of the cell.

cell wall a rigid outer covering found in plant cells.

chloroplast an organelle used by plants to make food from the energy of sunlight.

cytoplasm the jellylike fluid that fills the cell.

endoplasmic reticulum an organelle that makes proteins and lipids (fats).

enzymes chemicals used to break down food inside the cell.

Golgi apparatus organelle that sorts and packages useful substances for delivery around the cell.

lysosome a sac that contains digestive enzymes for breaking down food.

mitochondria organelles that convert energy from food into a form that cells can use.

nucleus organelle that directs the cell's activities.

organelle a small organlike structure with a particular function in the cell.

pseudopod a "false foot" that some cells use to move.

ribosome a part of the cell that manufactures proteins.

stem cell body cells that can turn into many different cell types.

vacuole an organelle used mainly for storage.

vesicle a package that carries useful substances around the cell.

www.ingramcontent.com/pod-product-compliance
Lightning Source LLC
Chambersburg PA
CBHW061257170426
43191CB00041B/2438